T0274908

Percussing the Thinking Jar is a marvel of ~~logs" make~~
~~logs" make~~ stream of consciousness feel ne ~~g~~ ~~~~ ~~~~ ~~og,~~
anxiety meditations, wild ideas: no idea or language is out of Win's
reach. This is original, gorgeous, engrossing poetry.
—Lee Herrick, poet laureate of California and author of *In Praise of
Late Wonder, New and Selected Poems*

Lately I've been worrying about poetic style, which is a branched
variation of the poet's perpetual subject of worry, language. Maw
Shein Win's *Percussing the Thinking Jar* took me a step away from
such worrying, weighted though the poems are with worry. Here are
poems in which a love of the sounds and textures of words is manifestly
a determining stylistic priority, poems that, consequently, are richly
musical, and feature lines that expertly play their rhythms against each
other—"vesper flux, pressure switch // I close my eyes & tap the lid."
How beautifully the ampersand in the second, iambic tetrameter line
both acknowledges—insofar as it is as much a symbol as a syllable—
and supplies the unstressed syllable missing in the first, not-quite
iambic tetrameter line! I'm grateful for that music, that style.
—Shane McCrae, *Pulling the Chariot of the Sun: A Memoir of A
Kidnapping*

Percussing the Thinking Jar is a multisensory experience befitting Maw
Shein Win, an artist who works and collaborates across disciplines
and genres. An inventive collection of "logs" recorded over several
years during and after lockdown, this book is a kind of Golden
Record, snapshots of a restless roving mind trying to make sense of
and connect to the world through personal and global cataclysms.
Here, the mundane mingles with existential fears, medical procedures,
contemporary art, apparitions of flora and fauna, and much more.

Piercing reflections ("I am blinking into another eye.") are juxtaposed with luscious phrases ("Vata & the Vine, Pitta of the Mind, Kapha & its Kind"), forming a haunting dreamscape that indeed "astonish[es] with sonic delight."

—Jenny Qi, author of *Focal Point*

Percussing the Thinking Jar is a breath of fresh air. A clarity. An order to the pandemonium of a global pandemic. Death becomes inescapable and each log constructs a life raft to navigate the uncertainty of being a body driven by its desire for aliveness. At any moment anything can happen, so why not let poetry happen? Why not fortify the isolated and aging body with "metaphor quarries"? With "hands [that] tremble quiet," Maw Shein Win offers observations that defamiliarize and sensate narratives that bring new value to our "post-capitalist worth." *Percussing the Thinking Jar* transforms human afflictions into a different organ for perception.

—Arisa White, author of *Who's Your Daddy?*

In "Thought Log about Thought Logs," the last poem in Maw Shein Win's book, *Percussing the Thinking Jar,* the poet begins: "I started writing thought logs in spring 2020/Response to isolation, scatter, containment." In her liminal poems, Win sensitively and precisely registers the pulse of living through the pandemic, alert to how daily life has changed, how magnified the smallest details have become, how "everything is phenomena," and how nothing can "last forever." Amidst the deaths and stillness, the nurse's instructions, shopping for "peanut brittle online," "mastering the art of doing nothing," and listening to "roadrunners," Win stays open to whatever the world throws at her, its gradations, shifts, and ruptures. This is a book to read and reread. It does something no other poetry book I have read does: it offers "diaphanous comfort" while we are at the "chaos party."

—John Yau, author of *Tell it Slant*

PERCUSSING THE THINKING JAR

Cover art: *Portrait of Maw Shein Win as Gertrude Stein* by Mark Dutcher
acrylic, glitter, oil on canvas, 2021-2023
back cover: *Painting for a Door* (detail) by Mark Dutcher
acrylic, oil on canvas, 2023
Cover design by Laura Joakimson
Cover typeface: Komet
Interior design by Laura Joakimson
Interior typeface: Garamond and Dapifer

Library of Congress Cataloging-in-Publication Data Pending
See https://www.loc.gov/

Published by Omnidawn Publishing, Oakland, California
www.omnidawn.com
10 9 8 7 6 5 4 3 2 1
ISBN: 978-1-63243-160-8

PERCUSSING THE THINKING JAR

Maw Shein Win

Omnidawn Publishing
Oakland California
2024

CONTENTS

>< = Drawing by Mark Dutcher

Thought Log

Swinging on an old rope from the edge of a cliff.

A lit-up room, a giant X covered in sequins.

Gone lawns, fan crowns, drone town.

An orange ceramic swallow from Portugal.

My love's laughter from the study.

Reimagine cures.

Amber nimbus, ochre hawks, spring shambles.

I believe in the healing power of crystals.

They thought my hair had turned white due to pandemic stress.

My sinuses are being occupied.

I feel lonely & then I don't.

I eat another bowl of kitchari, the bits of ginger.

Sorry fabric, mild steel, jade traps.

What are we in for?

The somatic therapist leads us on a guided visualization through a sacred grove.

I swim in a field of pathogens.

Thought Log

We prayed for calm instructions.

Uranium blue, Ultramarine, Glaucous.

A lolcat is a macro image of one or more cats.

Rag ants, blizzard glyph, foil punch.

What's below the iceberg?

Pitta eyes are sharp-bright, gray-green, light-sensitive.

Wild poison hemlock can be confused for Queen Anne's lace.

Feral carrot, edible wildflower.

Rote mutton, feel estate, mantel gardens.

Does our thinking affect what goes on outside us?

The auto correct of booster shot is buster shop.

My late uncle from Mandalay was a saboteur.

Helvetica, Sabon, Garamond.

Buried for discovery in future times.

I failed performance art as an undergrad.

Scorpio weed, parrot hands, pupil tremors.

Gazelle

sleeps near a tumbleweed

veins thumping soft

witness the neighbors in search of water

the cabin dwellers in fear of fire

what makes sounds at night: *nwack, nwack*

ringed horns, gaunt flanks

who takes a chariot to market

Sunday or evening, morning or March

young gazelle with bruised sides

licking water drops from a desert fountain

Stroke Log

and mereyo and alerafo and all yery alday

[Leaving out words like "is" or "the."]

will see my self, see if you and your, and see me, and yery

[Their sentences are illogical or don't make sense.]

A text my mother sent today.

[Acknowledge the affected part of their body as still part of the
stroke survivor.]

Her stroke.

Will see my self again

[Preventing brain tissue from getting oxygen
and nutrients.]

*yes, okay. Yes, I will try. If anytime you I from will let. we
any time you. we are going out from out from about us*

I look through texts.

[Reduce distractions by turning off the television, radio
or moving to a quiet place.]

I sent 15 photos of our cat to her in the last week.
This morning I hear a purr-mew
I swivel in chair
A patter notter

Bokchoy's not here

any more
any more

[Only talk about one thing at a time.]

We will see you all the time.
Please we will see you. Never
please we do. Always have
Bhokchok please

[Encourage the stroke survivor to fully scan their surroundings
to compensate for any loss in their field of vision or left-side neglect.]

Bokchoy's ashes in cedar box
Paw print in lace case

we will have
sumset   and pretty

Weather Log

where's dawn
she's at lexa's house
nerves permeate air

I visit with honeydew
last light dips through shutters
we make sourdough

wild saffron, swift wind
what is air, breath
crocus nest

yvonne's rusty locks
my brittle nails
meadow burns

gold flinches
look up

Dear H,

Dear H,
I'm hanging out in the waiting room. I am blinking into another eye, gold shades, sirens again. Seeing the city through the window of another window, I live in a two-second time lapse.

Dear H,
I stitched a quilt for you, slivers of green lint throughout. Warmth in the waiting room now, my limbs are soft with pain. Slept last night with ears open. Noted the following: pollen drift, vessel crack, pillar bark.

Dear H,
Missing your crackling eyes, generous fountains. And this: you were standing on a dock & next to you, a steamer trunk made of bone. Strangers began to gather. You sunk your hand & lifted a spinning plate from the trunk. Applause & more applause.

Dear H,
My cat visited me from the Otherworld. She witnessed bliss bursting from the pockets of houses open once again, bright light from the storehouse, tinny bell tones. She could smell the dirt from behind the shed.

Sleep Log

I talk while I sleep. Sometimes I laugh for a long while.

T tells me that I speak quickly & he can only hear my side
of conversations.

I dream about caves, lakes, drapes.

I flap my arms with much effort. Fly upwards, hit a smooth
white ceiling.

My snores are delicate, T says.

I hear a disembodied voice, snap alert.

For years, nails & shards of glass flew from my mouth. I imagined this
as rage.

Sleep under four heavy blankets.

Dream about losing a purse even though I don't own one. My
older sister visits me. She died six years ago. She swings a leopard skin
pouch around on a golden chain, she is glowing.

I whisper: everything is going to be okay.

Log Thought

read the vulnerability clause

faint in the trenches

find cheap healers online

I see a bluebird with teeth

I can't find my veins

my sister, an intimate contortionist

interrogate, vault

Log Thought

zippy lighter, milk tea, dumbbells

they had packed the essentials

unaware of blizzard

fleece suits, yes, cough drops, no

unprepared for slipping stones

fanged pandas, ice fauna

ascending slumber mountain

with fevered breathing

they flung the dumbbells off cliffs

drank tea from canteens of leather

exhaustion dreams, frostbitten limbs

rested against the elms that remained

slope, flicker

Kite Eye (or Eye Kite)
after a painting by Sylvia Fein

You look up at the sky. Ask questions. You see one eye. Or perhaps a kite. Must make a decision. You have one minute. Time almost up. An icecap melts. A spouse betrays. Buzzer goes off. Sun beams. You crack an egg. You marry an olive tree. Brightness arrives. Memorize adverbs of frequency. Look to the left. Taste of lingonberry. Swallow it whole. Painted frames. Forget answers. You ask for a horse. Camel vision. Lime bush. Copper artichokes. Vintage teeth. Kite eye.

Catalog

check work email, read about flooding in Puerto Rico, put lotion on dry legs, Spectravite vitamin bottles on dining room table, try to remember next PT appointment, listen to bird songs on YouTube, makes me think of the bird on yesterday's walk, my friend trying to ID with an app on her phone, the announcement by Taco Bell that their guacamole would not suffer from the impact of Mexico's dearth of avocados, where should I donate my clothes, picture my mother alone in bed at the monastery, the abbess in her kuti sending out newsletters on compassion, soldiers gun down village in Myanmar, text a client two close-up photos of the scars on my abdomen which I meant to send to my doctor at Kaiser: a thin trail of blood in one, the other shaped like a star, my navel exposed, my hand holding up my right breast.

Wetlands

Otter & mink roam the fen.

I don a vest of moss.

Cormorants, curlew, call from the bog.

I avoid the beehive.

Sea trout, croaker, swim through the marsh.

I consult my mood ring: how do I feel?

Sedges & saltbush, the bobcats are disappearing.

I cry at all the right times.

Observation Log
for Annabelle

warmed a nest
in my balmy palm
placed it back
in its gingko tree

                    turned aside & took rest for a while

Thought Log

Forest guardians, ox hair robes, pewter magpies.

What's working right now?

It's possible to be okay & not okay at the same time.

I lost my sizzle reel in the void.

Emerald swans, cricket satchel, yodel odes.

Identify the risk you're taking.

My log hears things I cannot hear.

My anxiety about disappointing my therapist.

Sclera, retina, macula.

We tend to not move in digital space.

I feel like a ghost haunting my own life.

Vata & the Vine, Pitta of the Mind, Kapha & its Kind.

Freed by our predictions.

I adore my boundaries.

Check the air quality index.

This will be the last time I use this sink.

Tympanum

A friend tells me she wants to live in a house with no light. Only rooms with walls she must touch to find the door that leads to the dirt path beneath invisible trees. Growing from a break in the brick.

+

A breakdown we live inside

Our eye-cell skin-cell finger-nail

They tell you to take a break

+

The child who lives upstairs runs. Sometimes she falls. She rarely cries. She doesn't stop. I lie in bed. Recovering. Tears roll into ears.

+

My eye had a breakdown

Of the take-a-break cell

eye, eye, eye

+

Look up

The floors have ears

Tympanum bounce

+

I'm on medical leave

Specialist says stare at a spot

Eye stare until eye blur

+

A spot on the wall observes action in the room. Moving glasses of water from one location to another. Night, fall. Hands make shadows. My ceiling, their floor.

+

The child who lives upstairs runs. Sometimes she falls. She rarely cries. She doesn't stop. I lie in bed. Recovering. Tears roll into ears.

Log Thought

forehead's thumping

hourglass flip

can you see, see me

can you hear, hear me

miracle vaccine

made in Burma

vein, machine

အတွေးမှတ်တမ်း

ခေါင်းထဲမှာ တဒုန်းဒုန်း
အချိန်တိုင်းသဲနာရီကို ပြောင်းပြန်လှန်

မြင်ကြရဲ့လား ကျွန်မကို
ကြားကြရဲ့လား ကျွန်မကို

တန်ခိုးကြီးတဲ့ ကာကွယ်ဆေး
ဗမာပြည်မှာထုတ်တာဟေ့

သွေးကြော၊ စက်

"Log Thought" translated into Burmese by Kenneth Wong.

Bokchoy Log

Bokchoy's green wicker ball with the bell inside rolls across the
floor.

I scan the living room. Silence.

Suddenly, a crow cawing. Rattling.

I leave our condo, walk to Giovanni's, buy an olive loaf.
An achievement.

Kidney disease. In her final month, I held up a small bowl
of water. Quick sips.

I move my hand to the seat cushion. Bokchoy's not there.

Photo on my phone: She is resting on the sofa, T touches her.

She'd sleep on my pillow & dream of birds falling from the sky.

Yesterday we saw an orange cat along the opposite sidewalk, mirroring
our movements.

Mom asks. I say, *We had to put her to sleep.*

A calico specter rests in the sun.

Stranger

Stranger than a trunk of beetles, a box of fur buttons.
My daughter is a stranger & I am a stranger myself.

We are strangers on a melting train. Sometimes she leaps
through the kitchen window while I bake zucchini bread.

Gretchen was a deer
Gretchen was a deer one year

My daughter is a hunter in the Black Forest.
Strange daughter, I hear you in my eyes.

Thought Log

Ephemeral locations rebroadcast on radio.

Sleep talk under a blanket of ice.

Amethyst tadpoles, rumble strips, sacred airspace.

We reconfigure our belief systems.

Discover the misting spot.

Share scream.

I catch the baby in the falling landscape.

I drop into my body & pay attention to the alarm system.

Our calico is shrinking.

Enshrine insights for future meetups.

We pantomime in distant rooms.

Smaze, foke, flare.

Hold open a space for coincidence.

Banana fellas, succulent pathways, butterfly farmers.

Flamadiddle, Ratamacue, Long Roll.

Stomped on the teleprompter.

Thought Log

Hula mantras, sacred optometry, lanai euphoria.

An island trickster disappears with a laptop.

Places with the highest daily reported cases per capita.

The memoir instructor: *Guts on the table, now.*

Testosterone descendants, anxiety gratitude, barrier echoes.

I conspired with the sun today.

Tom-tom, timpani, celesta.

The word-extinction capital of the world.

Our memory concussion.

All applause for the creator!

Orchid choir, wave scape, grass basket.

Fake meat pork chops & white rice.

The Earth's hottest years on record.

Found manifesto, desperation ceiling, storage unit.

The universal is personified.

Only wooden things always.

Finches

In the dream, the body runs from fire.
Throws on a cape, dashes through the door.
The body heads for the hills.
Overheard at a party: *Head for the hills.*

An ambulance speeds by, blur of rust.
Body informs mind: *emergency.*
Body tries to soothe mind: *breathe.*
Body sees a mother in a glass tank.

Water on the floor & feet cold.
Sometimes I forget I have a body.
A therapist once said that I did not have holes in my energy field.
My ex, however, had many.

In the dream, I have powerful legs.
My eyes are alert.
I fly over burning hills & flash floods.
Leap over hospitals & shuttered stores.

My body delivers a message.
Drink three bottles of ginger water.
My mother's body needs a walker, a hospital bed.
She reads in her dreams.

In the body of the dream, I am swimming.
A deep lake surrounded by firs & ferns.
Water soothes the mind.
Her body on a blanket of warm grass.

                              Books turn pages on their own.
                              Finches sleep in fiddleheads.

Observation Log

we hear chants

do their protests
sound out a future

we'll be able to witness?

my family in Yangon no longer
leaves home

မျက်မြင်သက်သေ မှတ်တမ်း

ငါတို့ ဆန္ဒပြသံတွေကြားတယ်

သူတို့မျှော်လင့်နေကြတဲ့
အနာဂတ်ကို
ငါတို့ မြင်ခွင့်ရပါ့မလား။

ရန်ကုန်က ငါ့မိသားစု အိမ်ပြင် မထွက်တော့ဘူးတဲ့။

"Observation Log" translated into Burmese by Kenneth Wong.

Hyphen Log

question mark-comma-hyphen
marks punctuated by division upon division

       a leaving-behind
       a coming-toward
       a moving-between

language heard over-tables under-walls
how we-connect how we-do-not

       flip-flops
       tea-shop
       full-stop

                         Burma-Myanmar

born within a-border is another-border

       collision-tables
       brain-sprain
       division-trains

a comma soft-pause separates conjunctions

       shot-echoes
       cyclone-pound
       plumeria-rain

The Thinking Jar

scorpion alert <> I wear

a cyan cloak

clock in at 10 a.m.

       cerulean frost on the

       found footage <> I see

       sea turtles in the subtropics

near the marigold altars

where elephants rest <> I light

a bayberry wick

53

Dome

That's not what she said, that's what I said.

The ants were everywhere.

In one conversation, a person speaks, another pretends to listen.

Takes place in a velvet chamber.

The ants take over the halls.

They circle the exits, fill sinks, crawl into politicians' ears.

One by one, people stop listening.

Ants skitter along cool tiles into the dome hole.

Stroke Log

roots awake from ash
small green shoots through ground
fan palm, yucca

my mother had a stroke
coptered from Joshua Tree to Palm Springs
we toss suitcases into the car

drive on the 5
pass a three-car accident
emergency vehicles arrive

lobelia & eucalyptus
lung curatives
burns darken the hillsides

incense cones in gold bowls, the surgeon calls,
my mother will have a thrombectomy
at the monastery, the samaneris chant

blaze burns young bark
smoke in the air
a PT says she can lift one arm

we call on the phone
wait, wait in friends' casita
110 degrees outside

my mother speaks in whole
sentences, can walk again
a miracle, says a nurse

redwood ash along the highway
look up from car window
heading home, sky space

three weeks later a second stroke
I board the plane alone
masked, anxious

return to the monastery
touch her dry hands
we listen to roadrunners

Thought Log

Dad knew he was going to die because he saw two vultures that morning.

Suitcases breaking open display queen conch shells.

Apparition of snapped bone trees.

Pataflafa, Flam Drag, Triple Stroke Roll.

The suburbs are sinking.

I record my mood shifts & flares in a notebook.

Floating holidays, cement memories, hot tub religion.

Dream bigger than an Airstream.

The neurologist will return in an hour.

Goat rentals for hillsides.

Identify your top three unhelpful thinking styles.

Surveillance jammer, sleeping lags, default salad.

Bloodline from a Burmese monarch.

My dentist used a percussion test to replicate my tooth pain.

Baby jumping, beetle fighting, extreme ironing.

Drink watermelon juice to quench your inner fire.

In another neighborhood

A honey possum darts across the floor of a downtown bar

among table legs, teachers, tourists.

In another city, a developer sets a building on fire.

The cabaret singer has bright teeth & a syrupy voice.

Eight elders wrapped in blankets.

Two tourists leave the honey bar.

The stand-up downs a shot of honey bourbon.

Survivors crawl into the emergency wagon.

Children play air guitar on trains for coins.

In another country, a woman sits alone in a kitchen.

Considers revolution, sips honey

wine from a glass chalice.

Sleep Log

I sleep wearing a long-sleeve cotton shirt. No underwear.

Dream: I live in a basement in Buenos Aires with other performance artists. If I want dinner, I am required to do a six-minute piece.

T snores deeply, soundly.

I dream about mini malls, stalls, fall balls.

We use silicone ear plugs from Walgreens. 12 to a box.

For years, my ex would appear. On a train, wearing a dark suit, moonlight on his face. Pretends not to see me.

T's foot seizes & he jumps off the mattress to walk off the pain.

Last night, a blue baby was sipping from a small bowl of Dr. Pepper.

Then, I run from a frenemy. She is a writer with fingers that trigger.

Long ago, a dream of granny in a flowery longyi. I cry in her lap.

61

Grapefruit Log

One year I ate a grapefruit every day.

+

My husband is allergic to grapefruit.

+

After surgery, I examine three scars on my abdomen, one above my navel, two longer incisions to the right and left. Wingspan of a sparrow.

+

My ovarian cyst was the size of a grapefruit. In 1964, *Grapefruit, A Book of Instruction and Drawings* by Yoko Ono, was originally published in a limited edition of 500 by Wunternaum Press in Tokyo.

+

Lying on the surgical table, heated blanket across my body, I remember the surgeon holding *The Complete Dramatic Works of Samuel Beckett*. Startling & comforting. In post-op, I notice he has shaved his three-inch beard.

+

CUT PIECE   from Yoko Ono's *Grapefruit*

> *Cut.*
>
> *This piece was performed in Kyoto, Tokyo, New York and London.*
> *It is usually performed by Yoko Ono coming on the stage*
> *and in a sitting position, placing a pair of scissors in front of her*
> *and asking the audience to come up on the stage, one by one, and*
> *cut a portion of her clothing (anywhere they like) and take it. The*
> *performer, however, does not have to be a woman.*

+

This morning, I check my wingspan in the mirror. Layers of healing, a disappeared bruise.

+

My friend gave me a grapefruit.

+

I sliced it.

Log Thought

mud jug, poison stream

    holding my head with my hands

anxiety spills, suspended atlas

    that time I got so high I, I

blurred pilgrims, rigged systems

    tossed across the room

immersive theater, verdigris promenade

    erratic visitations, my drawn-in brows

thorn, pheasant

The Thinking Jar

an antelope asleep in the wood
I shop for peanut brittle online
violet strings <> a muscle prediction

an airport therapy session or a clue
to find sea urchins in the beau
blue <> I draw with blood these days

a pile of pink shells <> I
am a dram of neurotic fixes
hatchling in the parlor

fingerling in the hot oil
fire ant eyes <> I drop a shock
of wicked white hair to the floor

a blackbird lands on the thinking jar
wonder if I can swim from the
isle of elderberry <>

Weather Log

scroll the gloom

the news blues

pour into etched goblets

elixirs of spirits

meditate with strangers online

suspended animation

what does it take to get out of bed

walk dazed toward coffee maker

our laptops hot pots

donate to charities

sleep through one night

winds rattle windows

       can't see ocean from here

       abounding in calms

       then quick sharp squalls

Towards No Earthly Pole
after a video by Julian Charrière

      erratic
      memory of sky

                when you're standing on the ice cap

                        punctured boulders where
                        moss fires glow green

               you're not standing you're flying

chop frozen entropy
milk fossils blue

Log Thought

stuck in the thicket, remote country

metamorphic coffins, I miss the palm

pinwheel move, sleeping wolf spiders

yawn explosions, I swipe away the muck

surcease, fronds

Log Thought

half-choked on a Brazil nut

I kayak when necessary

what shape is the sky

drench, blanch

Sensation Log

when you see it disappear

everything is phenomena : insect decline

no matter how pleasant

                        things are   they do not last

forever no matter how sad

or painful it is : can hear my mother breathing

doesn't last forever

                        if it continues   it will

be difficult for us to live

our entire life : we stayed in the comedy house

knowing it will come

                        to an end   someday we

live in hope of the next

if it is clearly understood : jars of water from a caregiver

rather than vaguely

                    aware there is   no more suffering

only when deeply rooted

ignorance is clearly ignored : a missing account

will delusions cease to arise

                    because its   roots are gone

Still

I stand still in the classroom corner

Wearing a paper dunce cap, balancing on one leg

Memory: knocking a pitcher of water off the countertop

Just to watch it shatter

Tonight I hear fireworks outside

Crackling the stillness inside

A thought: the story of a girl who had tumbled into a cave

& crawled her way out

Alive, quiet

I wear a red cloak to the 4th of July picnic

Stand still aside a pine tree

Three drops of sap land on my cheek

Focus my eye on a cave swallow until the fireworks end

Sleep Log

I drink a glass of water while sleeping.

Last night my dead cat walked through the air above me. I reached out to her as she disappeared.

I dream I am an orphan. I watch myself eating a hard-boiled egg over a metal platter.

I swallow a capful of Delsym Cough Syrup.

Rub my chilled feet against T's calves. My hands are cold too.

One summer I tried drinking heated milk with half cloves of garlic & nutmeg to combat insomnia.

I dream of moats, floats, old goats.

Every night we hear sirens & cars racing around the parking lots.

I ask T before he falls asleep in seconds, where should we meet?

If I wake in anxiety, I touch his back & count backwards in Spanish.

Thought Log

I visit my therapy horse once a week.

Loquat soup, badger prey, parlor lox.

Wipe us down with iodine.

Fawn corral, porch render, wardrobe blood.

Our intimate bubble state.

What some refer to as temptation bundling.

Surrender fully to the movement.

I undervalue my post-capitalist worth.

Monitor coffins, banister motif, creek ballots.

We unpack our elegance armor.

Is emptiness a placeholder?

Competitive landscapes, distilled manifestos.

The streams are disappearing.

How we find ourselves in metaphor quarries.

Poppy icing, hair weapon, chubby rain.

You're a something burger.

Vertigo

crystals in ears   head a snow globe   about to faint

is your vision doubled   can you walk   no I can't

slipping floor below   must pee standing up

wall spin   bed flop

painting shifts

+

move slow with intent   don't look up   don't look down

focus on spine of book: the word *delta*

call advice nurse   call 911   wait for ambulance

EMT guys arrive with gurney

blood pressure high

+

crystals are dislodged   floating in ear space

nausea   detachment   faint ringing in ears

fall forward   upper half of body collapses

face down   can't move

symptoms of other conditions

+

inside ear   tiny organ   labyrinthine

crystals break free   move in semi-circular canals

thin membrane   drum skins   a border between

hair-like sensors   send messages to brain

untether   unground

+

jade roller across brow   firm pillow below neck

EMT says can you stand   do you wear glasses   bring a book

lost balance   gone gravity   eye rolls

cortisol spells   are crystals pink

light   head

Observation Log

we live beneath
small pounding feet
think we're alone but
maybe we're dancing

I find a pearl & leave it on your doorstep

Hyphen Log
for rae

another night-night
or day-day
nomadic migrations

of cedar waxwings
circling-circles
above resilient hawthorn

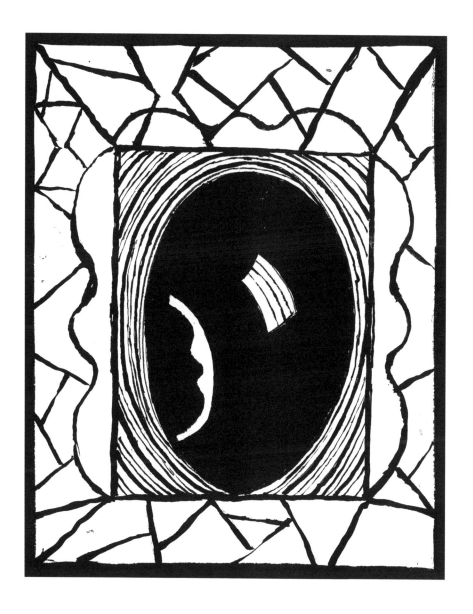

85

Blood Pressure Logs

aster revolution

brother stopped at the border

dying coral emporium

director calls: don't wear stripes

blood pressure: 130 over 88

sparrow hopping on one leg

blood pressure: 141 over 83

rigor hum, pastor spells

boss says: can you quit already

welcome to the chaos party

C & I go to Marshall's one week before my surgery date. I want something fuzzy to lounge in, new pajamas patterned with pink cats in space. Experience landfill guilt.

Last night I dreamt I was kidnapped by a health cult. The leader insisted I drink a potion made of crushed wood chips. I wanted to escape, then I wanted to stay.

The RN instructs: No Motrin, Advil, Aleve, ibuprofen. Tylenol, okay.

nurse advises: use tea bag as gauze

long for kind bones

fuzz trapped in the hollow

grunt crate

blood pressure: 127 over 86

dental technician digs

blood pressure: 138 over 94

flesh flotsam

life coach offers: never too old

crows brawl overhead

This morning I have my weekly writing date with A. She's wearing a knitted maroon cap. We share stories about medical procedures.

T & I take our blood pressure. 143 over 86, 150 over 94. Kaiser advises to sit up straight with feet on the floor, wait five minutes. Try again.

To-do-list: Download Calm app. Wash sheets. Pre-op vid appt. Buy stamps. Call HR. Lift weights.

I talk to my sister on the phone & ask her to make sure T is okay. She's annoyed. *Of course,* she says, *he's family.*

C & I go to a German deli in El Cerrito Plaza. The Junket. C orders a sundried tomato & cream cheese sandwich & I, a lentil avocado on sourdough. She tells me her cousin died of ovarian cancer.

popcorning on ether grid

blood pressure: 108 over 79

clover scrim, bee hair

sister whispers: avoid the cupcakes

a visit to fallout island

notice dew on whisker

boba cults

puppy fever galore

blood pressure: 119 over 81

neighbor reveals: time capsule found

My belly is round, hard. Size of a fortune teller's orb. An assistant takes my blood pressure three times. At the gynecologist's office, I reference that scene from the first *Alien*. The doctor doesn't smile.

I read that The Junket is closing.
Two words on the back of receipt: *Drink water.*

97

The Grisham House
for Adrian & Mark

it was velvet then noise
there was silence on sandpaper

I lived with an artist, a dancer, a sculptor
we drank Brown Derby beer

we lived by railroad tracks & talked to trains
sang among weeds & peach trees

my voice deepened an octave
the sculptor warmed up his explosion

we constructed a time capsule
buried it in the yard

I dropped in a poem, the artist a bottle cap
the dancer a polaroid of our house

yes, my octaves welcomed me
yes, I welcomed them back

Thought Log

We communicate via semaphore.

The neighbor boy stuck a wad of chewing gum in my hair. My mother rubbed butter on the clump to dissolve it.

A coalition of farmers in Central California.

The napes of our necks.

Red Clover, Ruda, Amarantus.

In the bowels of us they rumble.

Create new neurological pathways.

Suffering is wanting things to be different than they are.

Vesper Sparrow, Marbled Godwit, Vaux's Swift.

I download another meditation app.

Chemical cascades of gratitude.

I survived the Boxing Day Tsunami.

Thoughts can increase inflammation.

Brain pan, throttle mold, tinsel wreck.

Model the warrior pose.

Endorphins occupy my brain receptors.

Thought Log

I lift my furred paws toward my husband's face.

Child runs to hide in the teahouse.

Tapping over normal air-filled lung should produce a resonant percussion note.

Algophobia, androphobia, astrophobia.

Must wake to the pull of the outer world.

Researchers have found that cats can understand human pointing.

I-Want-To-Go-Home Theater.

Eye yam sew eggs awe stead thees daze.

Chuckle stern, breathing neck, blanket zone.

Get on the Ferris wheel.

I make spaghetti when I'm alone.

Slowdown in the supply chain.

Lumen parade, ginger chews, cooling pillow.

The triplets were born on a lavender farm.

Longyis, flip-flops, handmade shields.

An aggregate of robots.

Catalog

apply anti-itch cream on scar as if no one is looking, message from Dropbox that storage is full, jot down: *floating weeds, breakaway props*, worry about mom in hospital, doctor draining 1½ liters of fluid from her lungs, look up meaning of *shim* then *wild wall*, make turmeric ginger tea, text friend who can't move from bed, read about latest drive-by shooting, snip dead daisy petals, think of my students in Yangon unable to leave their homes, note number of white hairs falling on black sweater, remember found nest on last week's walk, write on back of envelope: *grief broke up visions of ourselves.*

Winter Hair
for Tom

I hear the songbirds more these days

try to decipher sirens & calls

you make a cocktail for us called *black lily*

I grow out my white roots, winter hair

our calico wails at 3 a.m.

my mother's losing her hearing

figs fall from nearby trees

a wild bobcat roams yards of shuttered homes

I read somewhere that blue jays molt

unkempt, they fly away

Thought Log

I experience sorrow in space.

Phantom smells, jock rockets, pod dwellers.

The Sutta advises the complete elimination of defilements.

An untimely breath.

How has that been working for you?

We remain speechless participants.

Bone tongue, sugar slots, sparse joggles.

Fact-check entities.

From inside, I can hear the tree cutters.

I quit Facebook & feel better now.

Pop-up armies, drizzle stores, butter trophies.

A group of devoted volunteers are knitting below the skin of my abdomen.

Archive of willow leaves in El Cerrito.

Joy tussles, forest cats, polka facades.

All of this is temporary.

On New Year's Day, we burn sage in the fire pit & twirl three times.

Vertigo Log

H sends a text on International Women's Day.

H has vertigo, third friend to come down.

I search *dizziness, vertigo, women.*

Read that empaths are suffering these days.

Illness, aging parents, overwhelm.

A student emails during class:

mentally burned out, can't focus

Earth revolves around sun.

Balancing act on axis.

Summer is winter, fall is spring.

Ground shifts below.

I bring mushroom soup to H.

Thought Log

Waiting for the light to sound.

My fear of moths, with their feathered wings & moving antennae.

Ribbon strips & handmade mask on driveway.

Once I made out with a stranger behind the Anti-Club in LA. He had a tattoo of an egg on his neck, odd but thrilling.

Muffin sheen, rust blouse, mushroom frost.

I am an optimist by nature.

The 18-year-old gamer in my voice-acting class can channel a cartoon poodle.

Ashwagandha, Triphala, Boswellia.

The tunnel of terror in *Willy Wonka and the Chocolate Factory.*

Our cat's fur falls in oily clumps. She caterwauls at 3 a.m.

If he stoops low enough, the river will too.

Grip flags, fake mud, duck stunts.

Mar's Magic cream on my neck & back.

Thoughts as objects, toppled monuments.

Someday After Moon Club.

The brilliance of crow at night.

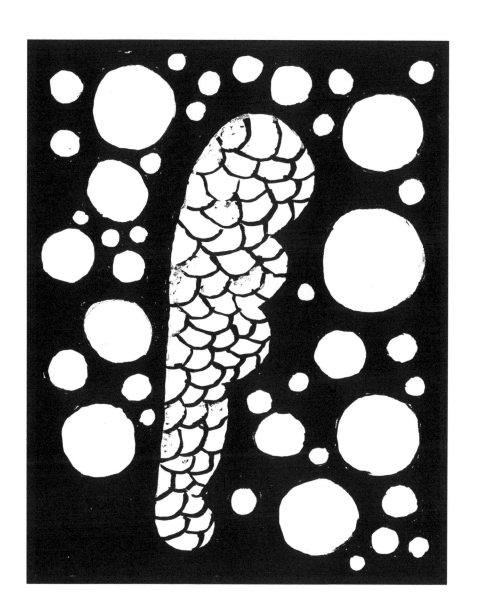

Syllabus Log

Module 1: Metaphor is a mystery of the human condition.

Imagine the compositional cloudburst.

No one has seen my lower half.

Module 2: Urgent offerings are hidden in banalities.

Subvert your attention.

We construct memories in 25-minute sessions.

Module 3: Implicate the readers to upend their views.

Astonish with sonic delight.

Teach 32 credits to begin climbing the seniority ladder.

Module 4: Visual rhetoric in relation to image skims water.

Include low stakes assignments.

My slideshow of falling architecture.

Module 5: Respond to nonce language with nonce enthusiasm.

Initiate labor-based grading.

Recurring dream of disappeared lesson plans.

Module 6: An examination of parlor flames.

Enliven the gestures of flat characters.

I revise my POV while brushing my teeth.

Module 7: How to archive lost scenarios.

Investigate the subjective experience of time travel.

Our field trip to the Pirate BBQ.

Module 8: Explorations of the vagus nerve.

Analyze relationships among air-breathing arthropods.

I grapple with squishy boundaries.

Module 9: Developing close underwater reading skills.

Inhabit painterly realms of the Otherworld.

Our pre-requisites lament.

Module 10: Ruminations on post-capitalist mindsets.

Engage with bamboo similes.

I loosen grip on desired income.

Module 11: Revision of initial response to pineapple jam.

Superficiality characterizes these "A+" essays.

Safe in our plastics, we develop enticing titles.

Module 12: How do we navigate intention & receptivity?

The body presents the "complication" that sets the plot in motion.

Review feedback on third nightmare.

Module 13: Unmask definitions of re-imagined disciplines.

Note that four absences will result in ailing chickens.

Differing types of engagement with leg veins.

Module 14: Some evidence of smelling strategies.

Students commit to deft aesthetics.

I long for counter-arguments.

Module 15: Division of product & process must be blurred.

Post-its of confessions on whiteboard.

Bring to class an object that fuses abstraction & glow.

Observation Log

on one walk
note flicker of
twigs & trickle
of stream

long jaw minnows swim a language

Thought Log

Live in a snow globe.

Gutter barn, iron lace, snake milk.

Short-circuited tank time.

I am made of soft bones.

Hurricane evacuation orders.

This is a testing situation.

Life can't kill my rainbow.

The year my identity was stolen.

Cinematic salmon tones.

Dream, boat.

Hot foam, pink snaps, mace stash.

I sense a donkey theme in the narrative.

Create calm corners.

Delectable lectures.

Raven bed, robe snatcher, bee wrangler.

We're having chocolate for dinner.

Thought Log

Frosted tea cakes for sale.

Pilcrow, interrobang, rubricator.

Swipe arnica across the hip.

Nat worship, village guardian, water spirits.

What do you notice when I say this?

Silence is my companion.

Meadow dots, god hobbies, odd goblets.

Continue to follow your department procedures regarding time off.

Dream house raffle snafu.

Stargazers, bulldozers, idolizers.

Paradigm shift or not.

Train rattle, rain tattle.

Liquidating savings.

I touch the velvet under the eaves.

Resonant, hyper resonant, stony dull.

Structure takes the panic away.

Catalyst
for Rusty

sphota: the existence of thought without words

a sac of skin is

a meaning sac

write from the neck

hole in the gut

fur on the arms

cold today

soft socks

back, ugh

note slow growth of eyebrows

warm germs slip

through the screen

into mouth-rooms

our gestural habits

legs know bed's

edge hands to banister

some dappled waters

silver tempers

paint   circles thought

123

Log Thought

the year they knew

to listen for

warplanes & windmills

not one or the other

empire, raze

Log Thought

the legalese was meant to confuse

hereby   whereby   therein

I named the country Passionland

cabinet, bite

Minnows

mist raven   felted forest   blonde moth

cauldron heat   ash casket

+

you   chop   zucchini
into   small   moons
from balcony drink in
a   digital   sunset

+

night glaze   brittle starlet   fox hoax

wooden grooms   milk baths

+

I passed you a cane
apple you made stone
pie matching scars
look inside our heads

+

throat currency   monster songs   strawberry tree

phantom cockpits   Odessa marquee

+

minnows speak in tongues
track   bright
you tend to obsidian wounds
we   sleep   in   circles

+

speckled fjords   sage farmer   ghost camp

bacon congee   fizzle chores

+

divvy up the light

Sky Garden

after a sculpture by Louise Nevelson

Photo of artist. Long cigarette in left hand.

Thick black eyelashes made of mink fur.

Shoulders cloaked in zig zags & embroidered dragons.

No smile.

         petite yet flamboyant

         On the streets of New York City, she collects castoffs.

            Table limbs, banisters, wooden planks.

          An architect of monochrome constructions.

              Grows a garden for the sky.

         the original recycler

Environment of wonder.

Living altar reveals nested objects.

Black acrylic paint tinted by shadows.

Shapes form visions.

black is the most aristocratic color of all

Cathedral of dreams.

Eight feet of surface drama.

Assemblage of echoes in wood.

Cast of crates.

we must create our own world

Sculpture stands & moves within space.

Rectilinear remnants, theatrical vestments.

Eyes travel across boxes.

Transforms detritus for the Otherworld.

131

Thought Log

Check the field notes before entering the rodeo.

I've been watching *The Age of Aquarius* on YouTube over & over.

Fish death, coiffed leaders, drought clock.

How can we propel you?

Back pain digs deeper but can't stop.

I dreamt that Ombretta got upset at a restaurant for giving her minuscule portions.

Eye shadows, chart pies, cinnamon dust.

The connection is unstable.

When I get nervous on Zoom, I start a conversation about hair.

What's alive in you right now?

They color coded their bookshelves for social media consumption.

Unpack those handsome artifacts.

Glockenspiel, monster costume, pork stock.

Articulate your topic space.

My digital portal is cluttered with kittens.

It's going to be a fold down winter.

Thought Log

King Dong, Lemon Oreos, unwashed scrubs.

Matching pinafores at the event that started with the letter M.

Three of my friends have fallen in the last three weeks.

Magpie music, magpie mirror.

Kerfuffle, skedaddle, paradiddle.

I am mastering the art of doing nothing.

Practice positive self-talk.

The ovarian cyst was defrosted for the biopsy.

Cinnabar, Carmine, Cordovan.

Utility pole with three metallic strips of yellow.

How do we experience diaphanous comfort?

Two children hawk objects on the lawn: wild daisies, toothpicks
wetly painted, neck brace.

We are 100% committed to hope at this moment.

My cousin's neighbor ripped down his decorative flower boxes
& hummingbird feeder.

Drill down into metaphor making.

Cutie Thunderstomp upstairs annoys & amuses us.

Blue Lines

        we walk around the block

        two masked bandits

        golden poppies burn our eyes

these days we count the pains

follow blue lines on charts

I ice my arthritic knee

        T cooks for us: yellow lentils

        red rice, warm squash

        take turns waking at 4 a.m.

from the second-floor window

I watch a woman below working

in her garden, weeding, watering

        wild rose & black sage burgeon

Bokchoy Log

BC's cat stand & cat bowl are empty.

Yesterday it rained & the sidewalks are cleared of blood, feathers.

Her ashes rest in a cedar box inscribed with her death date, paws imprinted in plaster of Paris.

A week later, a hummingbird feather blows across the floor.

I check under the table.

Fluffs of dust.

We scroll petfinder for cats available for adoption.

Sometimes BC enters my REM state. I awake, startled not to see her on the bed.

The grass on the lot for sale two doors over is a bright downy green.

Soft & welcoming.

137

Thought Log

Dawn is the opposite direction.

I dim from the outside, quiver on the inside.

Shrinking rivers, cleaving glaciers, stalling ice.

We met in a tasting parlor.

A woozy glow & a staggered motion noted from the home.

Sentence without verbs.

Rinse mouth with coffee.

Amber light radiates from turnpike.

Dance to XTC after dessert.

Fever aches, roti syntax, fluid rag.

Weather insurance is an untapped marketplace.

In a headspace I hardly imagined.

A drive-through testing center in Richmond.

Ghost hunting, duck herding, fork bending.

The leopard chased the fox via a dating app.

The zinnia twins have emerged.

Snake

Pain coiled within skull.

Spine serpentine on calfskin sofa.

Hydrocodone & THC bath salts from town.

Snake ascends from curving spine.

Grass gathers along forearms.

Foam brace holds neck up straight.

Snake in a patch near the crown.

Winding road ahead veers in the dark.

Musculoskeletal X-rays flash in brain.

Rip of ache zips from the hip.

Ginger & turmeric roots grow under scalp.

Rhizome shoots appear on shoulder blades.

Trance Log

We are writing from our dreams.
You close our eyes.
I hold one hand in the other.
We notice the topography of our palms.
Notice our lifeline has grown longer, our fate line shorter.

I see blood flow in channels from three scars on abdomen.
We itch.
Sense the flow along the torso, down the arm.
We hypnotize.
I see my sister's long fingers in our hands.

We face our palms upward.
I realize my lines have aged.
Hold our hands up to our faces, stay there.
I think about our sisters.
We touch their feet.

You write about our dreams.
I am not asleep.
We are in trance.
I stand to eat from my plate.
We sleep off the breadcrumbs.

Thought Log

Bring your attention back to the room.

Negroni, Cosmo, Gimlet.

Their disembodied voice.

Rosy starling probes for what's underneath.

Execute the reach.

Command Center, Charging Station, Body Doubling.

Draw a column of light in front of your spine.

Goblet of apple juice disappears from green screen.

They named their child Glypha.

Consider luck to be a viable option.

What could we have done differently?

Glazed limes, afraid nerves, stellar cellars.

Envision a benevolent universe.

Leyden jar, canopic jar, killing jar.

Feldenkrais decreases reactivity.

Plant another log on the fire of our burning love.

Forage

The foragers salvage front lawn lemons & fallen walnuts.
A leather saddle discarded on mown grass in El Cerrito.

Framed poster of Hans Bellmer's grotesque dolls.
The elements unravel & reveal.

Wild monkeys dash through downtown Bangkok.
Children scroll through Chromebooks.

Mansion dwellers on the hill cannot
stop baking: pound cake, beer bread, cinnamon buns.

The foragers wrap bright bandannas
tight across mouths.

The Thinking Jar

I dab viridian green on eyelids

a gnat hums <> in the factory

an opera is borne

on the shed an owlet

broods in shade <> I knit

a shawl of cadmium orange

blizzard blue swirls as

meerkats emerge <> I

swoon alone

amber sky space

I bathe <> in mint

a mole in the bush

The Thinking Jar

a raven in forest mist flaps
I sleep there <> land on silent feet
stricken leaves, loons asunder, white drunk eyes

a hand pockets yellow twig <> I coax deep star rebellion
strung with guts, frogmouths, my cavity family
specter of a father in thorn meadows, baptismal

a raccoon in the closet plays death metal
upstairs two people fall against iron wires
I am rose hybrid <> wet with the sweat of labor

a biscuit in butterflake motion
the casket <> sunset violet tendrils
I mold a beetle from warmed copper

a lighthouse in Iceland, I loosen my grip on snow
grey gripe <> trampled arabesque
censored by the library, a political leopard

a drowning in the river down state
I slide on the silty bottom
tawny coyote watching <>

147

Log Thought

atop crown

head dread

brain chain

I wear a mink cape

listen to 45 Grave

suck on a medicine pop

jaw clench

neck wrench

fall back to bed

spin, ponds

Log Thought

I remember nothing about

that day

little was said

I heard wind

then a river of

ice that extended across continents

ear, sting

Littoral Drift Nearshore #209
after a cyanotype by Meghann Riepenhoff

we're shoreline denizens
silt-blossom chrysanthemums

                              traced surfaces
                              photosensitive lit

scratched saline
sleet grays through

                    we snap blue sand around
                    my hand we faint a little harder

Stroke Log

from our second-floor window, I watch
the neighbor below, raking piles
of orange leaves, hair in a high bun

after my mother's second stroke, I tally
the lexicon that remains,
she monitors her blood pressure from afar

a friend paints a series called goth mountain
recalling failed utopias, I send
another three-line poem

an uncle sends texts all day, photos
of suits, glasses of wine, messages
to senators that unnerve

on a walk this morning, I see
our mail carrier, lean legs, fingerless
gloves, I offer gold-wrapped bonbons

                                        he accepts

Catalog

text caregiver Tiger Balm is on the way, listen to neighbor talk about the norovirus, drink water from a My Melody glass, stand on balcony, soak up sun, remember dad saying to mom: *have you taken a shower yet?*, regret repeating myself to T, stir fry white rice & two eggs for comfort, read news report on right-wing talk show host getting fired, hear high winds outside picture window, worry about flash floods in Rwanda, complete two sets of six side stretches, feel guilty about unanswered phone calls.

Dear L,

Dear L,

I am here in the kitchen, boiling eggs & chopping ginger.
Thinking of my ex & about the time he was obsessed with
making kombucha. That huge mother scoby floating in a bowl
& all those jars of amber kombucha taking up the counter
space. Remembering my dream last night: you were seven & I
was eight. We were trapped at the bottom of a cave. We could
see a hole to the sky from below. An occasional hawk would fly
overhead. We lived on onions & cabbage.

Dear L,

It's evening. I'm drinking nettle tea. Have you heard it helps with
hay fever? I thought you might find this amusing, especially
considering my multiple allergies, but I long to adopt a rabbit,
perhaps even two. I want to knit hats for them. Today I walked
all the way to the Rose Garden & wrote in my notebook:
Windermere, Escapade, Damask. How these names might be
suitable for rabbits.

Dear L,

Today I left my backyard cottage as the rain cleared. I needed to
breathe, enter the outside. I walked up Spruce to Grizzly Peak. A
squirrel dashed across my path, a plum in its jaws. I wore the pink
silk scarf you gave me on my birthday. I floated home.

154

Thought Log

Almond bangs, pasty babies, sparrow blurs.

Guilt pancakes at your service.

Mind shag, vein stud, botch cradle.

Neurosurgeon removes section of skull to access aneurysm.

Fear does not define me.

Attorney cat, loose mittens, trope harvest.

Smothered with feathers.

Color psychology for film directors.

A pots & pans protest, banging through the night.

Eel grass, pickleweed, cattails.

Computer code & the sickly world of soap operas.

Touch me, knot.

Does the writing shed light on the issue of mania curatives?

Capricorn underworld.

Scout locations for our punk rock retirement home.

Enter the magic outside.

157

You Cured Me, No, You Cured Yourself

I can see neighbors partying across the complex
felled shadows   tawny blur

can't make a decision
chimney swifts   percussing jars

I blow a goose horn, my bleeding gums
how do we ask for what we need

our bells are rattled now
time for self-interrogation

triplets or singles
flawed tender selves

hands tremble quiet now

Hyphen Log

how I love your ferret-flounder

your see-see-ball-action

your mesh-expansion

                I delight in your stick-figure-fashions

                your genetic-bacteria-drawings

                & Pandora's-Box-optimism

I adore your AI-voiceovers

Cochin-obsessions, shiitake-floorplans

murmur-rub-gallops

how I marvel at your smoky-ring-butt

lumber-baron-plumes

your say-something what-are-you-thinking-of

wonder at your buzz-whip-dance-numbers

ambient-screams, saturated-moans

montage-sugar-shots

      my monofilament-puff

      how you-I, how I-you

      how I-I, how you-you

Thought Log

We reside on Agoraphobia Boulevard.

Sleigh meds, magnolia waves, brain tease.

Headaches behind the right ear for two months.

Someone on a bike yells at us for wearing masks outdoors.

I take a selfie while doing a restorative yoga pose.

Chain dimples, owl kitsch, cheese lust.

Document your inner landings.

Drifting again.

Lemon rinds glazed in sugar dust.

Are we looking for a specific response mechanism?

Sweep the velvet off the leaves.

We've entered the ringlet environment.

Bloke trolls, logo mills, cure oils.

I point my flashlight toward the charms.

How do we allow ourselves back inside?

Even the emojis are aging.

Thought Log

My eyelashes are falling out, one by one.

Yellow spiders, feral plumbers, folly poppies.

We experienced an understated turmoil.

Evidence of future life forms.

Marshmallow blooms in creepy cul-de-sac.

Thought they saw a dagger in his side pocket. Lint glint.

I want to make a living playing air drums on YouTube.

How has this department contributed to your personal
& professional growth?

My astral body hit the panic button.

Cortisol valleys, snuffer wax, bubble flicks.

My husband grew up on Inspiration Drive.

K-pop signature moves.

Optima, Ultima, Univers.

How do we fold into each other?

Memorize suborbital flight patterns.

Drowning in honey.

Torsion

My right ovary, an egg desert.

Fortnight Lily, petal armor.

Uterus, container of blood memory.

Left ovary, mourned bud.

Swallow pain, sink in tub.

One perfumed fibroid, rock melon.

Remove seed pods from cervix. Bouquet effect.

Floating frond, an enigma in the canal.

Disorderly array of tissues, tendrils.

Blooms in blackness.

Entries

hello nightlight
hello schemer

I feel a shift under the chair
I drape then dollop

I restore my surface
with blue & green stitches

entry:

apple core, rust towel, carving spoons
wolf pouch, cap racks

I smell trouble born

I am lichen
I darn then damage

sleep on a pixel quilt
quit my job before it begins

entry:

sugar scrub, joy gush, dorsal spin
popper lock, snow lake

I go salmon shopping

when I was six, I wandered into a virtual valley
I dropped then dripped

near the flood on the asphalt
I saw liquid tricks

       entry:

       dizzy blister, sunny buckets, timber knocks
       uncle's teeth, blaze swells

       I keep my distance from the cult

I have a hidden life
I disco then distill

blankets are dresses these days
I lick my palms dry

       entry:

       vortex drift, amber chamber, water rabbit
       ox feathers, chatter head

       I am introspective paradox

a jade swan
I dapple then dipstick

watch the royals flash their pretty forks
I am my own clone for now

goodbye trumpet of death
goodbye softie

entry:

chanted robes, dauphin beaver, vested beasts
vesper flux, pressure switch

I close my eyes & tap the lid

Notes

Thought Log about Thought Logs

I started writing thought logs in spring, 2020.

Response to isolation, scatter, containment.

I write by hand; I type.

Dreams, nightmares, observations.

Juxtapositions, found language, entries.

An attempt for order in the clearinghouse.

Each thought log has 16 lines.

Phrases come in threes.

Fever aches, roti syntax, fluid rag.

Sometimes a question:

How do we fold into each other?

Fragment: Waiting for the light to sound.

Observation: They color coded their bookshelves for social media consumption.

Instruction: Check the field notes before entering the rodeo.

Sensation: I'm drowning in honey.

Mantra: Life can't kill my rainbow.

Process note by **Mark Dutcher** on the art in *Percussing the Thinking Jar*:

My 16 Sumi ink drawings are a visual language of symbols that are a direct response to the poems in the collection. The main symbol being the witness, an observer who appears as an eye that is logging thoughts, seeing joy, counting anxieties, worrying, and feeling love. Other symbols that appear are the hourglass, a wing, a face that is a vase, utopian mountains, memory holes, and brain waves.

Cover image:
Portrait of Maw Shein Win as Gertrude Stein
39" x 32"
acrylic, glitter, oil on canvas
2021-2023

Back cover:
Painting for a Door (detail)
94" x 59"
acrylic, oil on canvas
2023

Bio
Artist Mark Dutcher brings together elements of abstraction, Surrealism, and Pop in paintings that incorporate layers of words and symbols, imprecisely rendered and frequently illegible. Often sampling song lyrics or names of former loves in his rough-hewn paintings, Dutcher explores notions of transience, loss, and death. He leaves blemishes and fingerprints visible and mistakes intact, emphasizing the artist's hand and process. "I'm interested in flaws and systems that leave flaws, in the traces that demonstrate that things don't always work out the way you think they will," he has said. Dutcher experienced the loss of a partner and of friends during the AIDS epidemic, and his work has obliquely addressed these personal traumas. Influences on his practice include the work of the Russian avant-garde artist Alexander Rodchenko and the California

artist Richard Diebenkorn. He lives and works in Los Angeles and The Sea Ranch, California.

Process note by **Kenneth Wong** on translating short stories and poetry from Burmese to English:

When translating, I strive to remain faithful to the original text—the mood it conveys, the sights and sounds it describes, and the metaphors it employs. What I often have to overcome is the vast cultural and linguistic differences between East and West. The ogres, the mythical birds, the Buddhist parables, and the quintessential Burmese expressions in the original cannot directly be translated into English, so I have to find comparable creatures, imageries, Biblical stories, and idioms to bridge the gap. The process usually reveals why people from different backgrounds have trouble communicating with one another.

Bio
Kenneth Wong is a Burmese-American author, translator, and language teacher. Born and raised in Rangoon (Yangon), Burma (Myanmar), he currently lives in San Francisco, California and teaches Burmese language at UC Berkeley. His essays, short stories, articles, and poetry translations have appeared in the *San Francisco Chronicle, AGNI, Grain, The Irrawaddy, Myanmar Times*, Two Lines Press, *Portside Review*, and *The Journal of Burma Studies*, among others.

The translation for *Percussing the Thinking Jar* in Burmese is

အတွေးပုလင်းကို တီးခေါက်ကြည့်ခြင်း

Notes for ekphrastic poems

Kite Eye (or Eye Kite), after a painting by Sylvia Fein

Sylvia Fein: Kite Eye (or Eye Kite), 2006
https://bampfa.org/program/sylvia-fein-matrix-275

Vata & the Vine, music by Evan Karp
https://other-people.bandcamp.com/album/after-sylvia-fein

Towards No Earthly Pole, after a video by Julian Charrière
Julian Charrière: Erratic, August 6, 2022–May 14, 2023, SFMOMA
https://www.sfmoma.org/exhibition/julian-charriere-erratic/

Sky Garden, after a sculpture by Louise Nevelson
Sky Garden, 1959-1964
https://anderson.stanford.edu/collection/sky-garden-by-louise-nevelson/

The Thinking Jar : : : I dab viridian green on eyelids
Originally inspired by four small book paintings by Linda Saccoccio for her ekphrastic collaboration project.
https://www.lindasaccoccio.com

Littoral Drift Nearshore #209, after a cyanotype by Meghann Riepenhoff
Littoral Drift Nearshore #209 (Springridge Road, Bainbridge Island, WA 02.12.15, Fletcher Bay Water Poured and Fletcher Bay and Fay Bainbridge Silt Scattered), 2015

https://www.sfmoma.org/artwork/2016.520.A-KKK/

Acknowledgements

Much gratitude to the editors and staff of the following journals and anthologies in which some of these poems have appeared, sometimes in different versions: *The American Poetry Review*, *The Margins* (Asian American Writers' Workshop), *The Bangalore Review*, *Poetry Daily*, *Swwim*, *Oversound*, *MumberMag*, *Antiphony*, *100 Word Story*, *BlazeVOX*, *Lantern Review*, *West Trestle Review*, *Traffic Report* (Small Press Traffic), *Portside Review*, *Dusie*, *The Banyan Review*, *Touch the Donkey*, *parentheses*, *Interlitq*, *The Racket*, *Spotlight Series*, *Trilobite*, *Maintenant*, *Omnium Gatherum Quarterly*, *Poem-of-the-Day* (SFPL). The following anthologies and projects published *Dear Human at The Edge of Time: Poems on Climate Change: : Poems on Climate Change in the United States* (Paloma Press), *Pandemic Puzzle Poems* (Blue Light Press), *A Home in the Bay* (Aunt Lute Books), From Collective Isolation: Poetry in Response to the Pandemic (BAMPFA), *Colossus:Body* (Colossus Press), *Mark My Words*, a collaborative artist book with Elizabeth Sher, *A Shape Produced by a Curve* (great weather for MEDIA), *Made Here* (Arts Research Center), Manifest Differently (Clarion Alley Mural Project), *The Plague Edition of Konch Magazine*, KALW: Bay Poets, and the APICC (Asian Pacific Islander Cultural Center) USAAF 2024 Festival. "Thought Log about Thought Logs" was originally published in the *ottawa poetry newsletter*, curated by rob mclennan.

Heartfelt gratitude to Rusty Morrison for her vision, editorial advice, and support of my work and so many others. So many thanks to Laura Joakimson for her beautiful work, patience, and generosity, as well as to the Omnidawn family. I'll always be grateful to Ken Keegan for his dedication and amazing work. Abiding thanks to rae diamond, Becca Black, and Amanda Williamsen for their careful reading of this manuscript and their encouragement. I could not have completed this book without their poetic brilliance.

Enormous thanks to my beloved writing groups and partners: Lynne Barnes, Heather Bourbeau, Christopher Cook, Heather June Gibbons, Connie Hale, George Higgins, Kathleen McClung, Vince Montague, Peggy Morrison, Trisha Peck, Paul Quin, Elizabeth Robinson, Lisa Rosenberg, Anne Walker, Audrey T. Williams, and Rachel Zarrow.

For their friendship, inspiration, and support: Sara Biel, Karla Brundage, Yvonne Campbell, Aileen Cassinetto, MK Chavez, Liz Costello, Emily and Ken Duffy, Michelle Dunn Marsh, Grant Faulkner, Lourdes Figueroa, Sylvia Fox, Steve Gilmartin, Lael Gold, Lillian Howan, Glenn Ingersoll, Susan Ito, Annice Jacoby, Evan Karp, Nathalie Khankan, Martha LaMair, Thirii Myo Kyaw Myint, Grace Loh Prasad, Alex Mattraw, Shikha Malaviya, Linda Norton, Jim Oberst, Ethan and Annabelle Port, Connie Post, David Ross, Pam Shen, Kim Shuck, Chris Stroffolino, Kimi Sugioka, Lydia Sviatoslavsky, ko ko thett, Megan Wilson, Kenneth Wong, Tim Xonnelly, and other fabulous friends in community.

Thank you to rob mclennan, editor and publisher of *periodicities: a journal of poetry and poetics* who features my Process Note Series and to all contributing authors. Continued gratitude to all the talented writers and poets at The Writers Grotto and Rooted & Written. Thankful for the arts and literary communities and spaces in the San Francisco Bay Area, poets and writers, organizers and curators, editors and publishers, bookstores and art spaces for their continued commitment and dedication.

Special thanks to Dawn Angelicca Barcelona, Mary Volmer, and to everyone who supported Maker, Mentor, Muse. Much appreciation to my teaching colleagues and students.

To my sister Thet Shein Win, thank you. Much love to my mother Ayya Gunasari and to my family and extended family.

Forever grateful for my longtime friendships with Mark Dutcher and for his gorgeous paintings and Sumi ink drawings for this book and to Adrian de la Peña who continues to inspire me.

Thank you to Bokchoy, my fierce and beloved calico and companion of 19 years.

As always, so much love and appreciation for my partner in time, Thomas Scandura.

Thank you, reader.

Photo by Annabelle Port

Maw Shein Win's most recent poetry collection is *Storage Unit for the Spirit House* (Omnidawn) which was nominated for the Northern California Book Award in Poetry, longlisted for the PEN America Open Book Award, and shortlisted for CALIBA's Golden Poppy Award for Poetry. Win's previous collections include *Invisible Gifts* and two chapbooks, *Ruins of a glittering palace* and *Score and Bone*. She is the inaugural poet laureate of El Cerrito, CA. She teaches poetry in the MFA Program at the University of San Francisco and was selected as a 2023 YBCA 100 Honoree. Win often collaborates with visual artists, musicians, and other writers and her Process Note Series features poets and their process. mawsheinwin.com

Percussing the Thinking Jar
by Maw Shein Win
Cover art by Mark Dutcher
Cover typeface: Komet
Interior design by Laura Joakimson
Interior typeface: Garamond and Dapifer

Printed in the United States
by Books International,
Dulles, Virginia on Acid Free Archival Quality Recycled Paper

Publication of this book was made possible in part by gifts from Katherine &
John Gravendyk in honor of Hillary Gravendyk,
Francesca Bell, Mary Mackey, and The New Place Fund

Omnidawn Publishing Oakland, California
Staff and Volunteers, Fall 2024
Rusty Morrison & Laura Joakimson, co-publishers
Rob Hendricks, poetry & fiction editor,
& post-pub marketing
Jeffrey Kingman, copy editor
Sharon Zetter, poetry editor & book designer
Anthony Cody, poetry editor
Liza Flum, poetry editor
Kimberly Reyes, poetry editor
Elizabeth Aeschliman, fiction & poetry editor
Jennifer Metsker, marketing assistant
Katie Tomzynski, marketing assistant
Kailey Garcia, marketing assistant
Rayna Carey, marketing assistant
Sophia Carr, production editor